Hurricanes, Paradise and Fairy Tales

By

Kim Norris Samuels

This book is a work of non-fiction. Names and places have been changed to protect the privacy of all individuals. The events and situations are true.

© 1996, 2003 by Kim Norris Samuels. All rights reserved.

No part of this book may be reproduced, stored in a retrieval system, or transmitted by any means, electronic, mechanical, photocopying, recording, or otherwise, without written permission from the author.

ISBN: 1-4033-9624-8 (e-book)
ISBN: 1-4033-9625-6 (Paperback)

This book is printed on acid free paper.

1stBooks - rev. 02/05/03

Dedication

This book is dedicated to all of my angels that watch over me: Mommy, Daddy, Dawn, Ronnie Jr. and Aunt Jean. Thank you for your constant guidance.

Love Always,

Kim

Hurricanes, Paradise and Fairy Tales

St. Maarten September 1995

Pristine beaches with white sand and crystal clear light blue water; rolling green hills get kissed year round with warmth and sunshine. Palm, Mango, Banana and Flamboyant trees are in my yard. The beauty of daily sunsets and nightly appearing stars is calming, healing and revitalizing. This is the Caribbean, my home.

Have you ever been on vacation to a tropical island and not wanted to leave? Wished you could make it your permanent residence? Well, I'm there! I get to see and enjoy the beauty, the magnificence daily. It's rough, but somebody has to do it! Stuck in traffic? So what, nine times out of ten you still have a view to die for!

I always knew that I was not destined to live in cold weather. Snow is not my friend. Sure, as a kid, it's great to play in, but the novelty soon wears off. I do like to watch it on television now, though. I don't believe I could ever live in a metropolis again (notice I didn't say "never" - never say never. You're only tempting fate!). I'm quite laid back now, plus my blood has thinned. Some people don't understand that statement "my blood has thinned." It is totally true that once you become acclimated to this warm climate, cool will seem like freezing.

I feel like I am living a dream come true, a fairy tale. How many people would love to be in my shoes? A lot. I know I am fortunate. I don't take my surroundings for granted for one minute either. I know that I live in paradise.

As they say though: "You have to take the good with the bad…."

Everyone has seen some natural disaster on the news at one time or another. When we see the gruesome aftermath, we shake our heads and say "Oh my God, that's horrible." You cannot even begin to fathom the events that had to be experienced to get to that end. Sure, you might try to imagine them, but, believe me when I tell you that whatever you could possibly conceive of is only about ten percent of what the actual being there is truly like.

In summary: You don't have a clue!!

Kim Norris Samuels

Monday September 4, 1995

My husband Ronnie and I woke up. We knew that this was not just "another day in Paradise". Hurricane warnings had been issued during the weekend and Hurricane Luis will be affecting us by tomorrow. I wished Ronnie a Happy Birthday. That sums up his gift. I had previously planned to go buy him a watch today and take him out to dinner, so much for that. There were far more urgent items on the agenda. Besides, all money on hand had to be rationed. Plywood was the priority. We needed it to board up the windows. Luckily, (if you can call it that) we were pretty well stocked with canned goods, non-perishables, candles, drinking water, clean clothes, batteries etc. There was a tropical storm warning (Iris) last week that we had prepared for, but it turned away from us. Ronnie insisted that he had a gut feeling that this time it would not turn away and it would be bad. Yet, he was amazingly calm. I assumed he didn't want to scare me more than I already was. This tactic was not working.

It was a complete madhouse on the road. People were scurrying around like rats for that last piece of cheese. The lines in the stores were horrible. In the hardware store we needed more nails, masking tape for the windows, and saw blades (I didn't know what the saw blades were for). While in line there was a rain shower outside, making us aware that this was indeed for real. The people were in the store discussing things like how much money the stores were raking in and asked, "what if the hurricane passes us? All of this money will have been spent for nothing!" I thought to myself, I hope that it would be for nothing.

Then you had the naïve people that were under the delusion, "It's not coming here and I'm not going to do anything extra to prepare." Reiterations of "St. Maarten has been lucky in the past so..." could be heard. Did people believe that those misguided ideas were going to ward off an act of Mother Nature? It boggled the mind.

Ronnie's parents had been visiting with us in St. Maarten since July and it was usually their custom to stay until after his birthday. Originally, they were booked on a flight leaving for New York on September fifth. The previous Friday, having heard reports of a forecasted hurricane, Ronnie had changed the reservation to the fourth. They were confirmed. That morning American Airlines advanced the flight time from four in the afternoon to noon because of the impending weather. Other visitors that had not changed flights earlier would now be stuck here to literally "weather the storm". They kissed us goodbye and drove themselves to the airport. We didn't have a minute to waste to finalize our preparations. Thank God the in-laws were able to get out. Not only and primarily for their own safety, but it was two fewer persons to worry about. My nerves definitely couldn't take the additional strain. Not only did we have to worry about ourselves and our house we also had two apartments with tenants, in our yard, to oversee. Since this property was all a part of our responsibility, it was already overwhelming.

The plywood was delivered while Ronnie went to a coworker's house to pick up steel rods. Upon his return I was instructed how to cut these rods (now six feet in length) into twelve-inch pieces. This was done with a hacksaw (now I knew what the saw blades were for!). These rods will be used to secure the plywood over the windows. The expression on my face pretty much summed it up, but still I said, "You have got to be kidding!" I got a glass of wine to get ready for all of this muscle work. After I had been sawing and sawing and sawing some more I completed six pieces. My arms felt as if I had just pitched a major league baseball game! Just out of curiosity I asked, "how many of these do you need?" He was doing calculations in his head and his lips were moving but nothing was coming out. Finally, he said "about thirty-six."

"Thirty-six! Thirty-six! Have you lost your mind?" I ever so nicely and demurely responded. Well, this seemed like a good "wine refill" break for me… O.K. I was ready to go again. Sawing, sawing, sawing. Forty-five minutes later I was almost finished, when one of my tenants came over with a steel cutter. "Why don't you use this? It's much easier!" Well, my eyes started bulging, my mouth was somewhat askew - it was not a pretty picture. He said, "I'm sorry, I didn't notice what you were doing until a few moments ago." I was ready to kill everyone just about then, so I just went in the house and let them finish the last few pieces. I was still in shock that I had actually done all of that manual labor. Who knew there was an easier way? Time for another wine break and to regroup.

Three o'clock. There was a strong, stiff breeze blowing.

Ronnie was finishing plywood patrol, measuring and sawing while Shari (my ten year old stepdaughter) and I started to tape the windows. You may have seen this done before. Usually, the tape is put up in an "X" fashion so that if the glass breaks it won't project inward, causing injury. Well, Miss Shari was sooo neat, her windows looked like graphic designs. Mine, on the other hand, looked like a monkey put the tape up! My hands didn't seem to be cooperating. O.K., time for another wine break. You think all this wine has something to do with my problems with the tape? Before you answer remember I just sawed all of those steel rods. If Julia Childs has wine while she cooks surely I can partake while I prepare for a hurricane.

Next, I started to take down mirrors, pictures, and put knick-knacks away. I didn't really know what I was doing and I wasn't sure what should be put away. I played it by ear as I went through the house. Hurricane lists give you generalities of things to do, like: put valuables in a water proof container, fill the tub with water, fill your car with gas, have cash on hand, stock up on batteries, candles, drinking water, canned goods, ice, and non-perishables. These are the common sense things most people could figure out. It's the little things that someone should make people more aware of, like you'll soon find out. I understand that in doing so it may tend to heighten someone's fear more, since they don't want to imagine things being that bad. The feeling of the unknown was strong and you felt so vulnerable. I'm not positive that I described this feeling to you correctly, but it was very unsettling. You're already moving on automatic pilot but there is this constant gnawing at you of "what haven't I done that I need to do?" Anyway, I arranged candles, flashlights, batteries and the radio for easy access once the electricity went out. I filled some pots and pans with water and put them in the bathroom for flushing purposes. O.K. Now it's time for another wine break. You have to pace all this work you know!

Since the dogs would have to be inside I got them ready for a flea and tick dip. We had a Rottweiler named Ricky, a Rottweiler/Doberman mixed dog named Lucy, (what kind of a crazy household could be without Lucy and Ricky?) and a mixed Shepherd named Hammer (don't ask). This bathing was extremely strenuous. They were moving around so much that half of the flea dip got on me. So, three dogs later and with myself now included as a dip victim, I finally finished. Well, at least I had one less thing to worry about; I was also flea and tick free!

Ronnie finally finished installing the plywood over the windows. His muscles were like putty. He was spent and so was I. (It's not that he hasn't been working hard all of this time while I have been describing my escapades, but his chores are just not as interesting!) We took time for a hot bath, watched some television, and tracked the hurricane up-dates, which were not promising. The storm was headed straight for us and worse yet, had slowed down tremendously. It looked ominous enough on the weatherman's chart and difficult to envision it as a reality. Not suprisingly, the wind had begun sending keen blasts against our safe domain. We attempted to get some much-needed sleep.

This is a very long way from Queens....

1963

My mother, Joan, my brother, Keith - six years old and I, Kim (four years old) had just moved from East Patterson, New Jersey to St. Albans, Queens. It was a nice, quiet middle class neighborhood. James Brown, Count Basie, Jackie Robinson, Roy Campenella and Brook Benton had homes within walking distance.

We lived next door to my Aunt Lynne and my first cousins, John and Dawn. My aunt and my mother, the only children of John and Elizabeth King, were both teachers, following in their father's footsteps. Dr. John B. King, was my grandfather and the first Black Deputy Superintendent of Schools in the New York City Public School system. We spent our summers at his beach house in Sag Harbour (now it's the "in" place for celebrities. Been there, done that.)

Our neighborhood was chock full of kids playing non-stop. We played double dutch jump rope, hot peas and butter, hide and seek, hop scotch and punch ball. We were never stationary for very long and you would have to drag us into the house, though, we knew that when the streetlights came on you had to go inside.

Being new in the neighborhood, my mom inquired about childcare. A woman was recommended that lived three blocks away from us. She was great with kids. There were also three children - Clayton, Wanda and Ronnie (he was five) that lived right next door to her, more playmates.

Eventually, I ended up spending a good deal of time at Ronnie's house, too. I became as much a part of his household as he was. Ronnie and I became bestfriends and his mother "Aunt Margie" became my second mother. She taught me how to sew, bake and ride a two-wheeled bike. She also became my mom's best friend. Ronnie was my protector and I was quite cocky knowing that he would always be there for me. Yes, sometimes I would even instigate altercations. He knew I did, but he did not feel used. He knew that I liked knowing that he was always there for me. We had always told each other practically everything, too. Whenever my best girlfriend, Michelle, and cousin Dawn wanted to go to a show or the movies Ronnie, had to go in order to watch out for us, like a bodyguard. It was just the way it was when we were kids.

My mother got married for the second time. He was a Funeral Director named Jack Duncan. (He was a close friend of Adam Clayton Powell and he even resembled him.) His two sons also moved in with us. I was about eleven at the time and they were three and four years older. The "happy" marriage did not last long before physical abuse reared its ugly head. I could remember cringing under my sheets with my hands over my ears to block out the yelling and hitting sounds. It was only a matter of time before my brother and I was to be included in these festivities. We would sustain a swift hard back handed slap if we caught my stepfather in the wrong mood. One instance in particular stood out. I got slapped so badly that there were welts across my face and marks left from his hand imprint. It wasn't long after that incident that my mother had to get stitches in her lip. (Her teeth had been punched through it.) She left him.

A few years later, I told Ronnie that one of my stepbrothers had repeatedly sexually molested me (not full penetration but close enough). "I'll kill you if you tell anyone", my stepbrother said to me all the time. My mind had done a good job of repressing the memories until I could deal with them. My mother overheard part of my conversation and called me to speak with her. She was distraught to say the least, but thankful she had gotten all of us out of a very bad situation. If she hadn't overheard me I don't know if I ever would have told her.

That nightmare being over, I went on to Jamaica High School and so did Ronnie. We went slightly separate ways during this time but never grew too far apart. I was busy on the cheerleading squad and he was working after school. I fell in love with a basketball player and got married a year after graduation, in 1977, at eighteen years old. Ronnie was at the wedding. He got married the following year and I was at his wedding. I gave birth to my son, Jeffrey on March 18, 1980 and Ronnie's son was born on (the same day as me!) May 10, 1980. We visited often so they grew up knowing each other.

My marriage differed from my mothers only because the abuse I sustained was verbal. I went into a shell, having no self-confidence and little self-esteem. My friends didn't recognize me. I was not my former happy self. I became a hermit when not at work and rarely spoke to anyone, except my husband's family. To keep me under control he involved "us" with the Pentecostal Church. Then, he conveniently had other things to do. So, I was busy in the Church and he could do as he pleased. There I was, doing everything he planned out for me. He now had my spare time taken care of. When I was at Church he would be off to some event or another, all bogus of course. Years later, I finally contacted Michelle and told her what was going on. I told her the "stories" he would tell me to explain his whereabouts. She tried to talk some sense into me. I wasn't listening. I wasn't ready to accept what was happening. One day she just screamed at me "would you wake up and smell the coffee!" I finally saw everything for what it was but was not yet ready to give up.

Ronnie had gotten a divorce and moved to St. Maarten (where his grandparents were born) in 1981. In the meanwhile, I stayed married another two years before the foreseeable demise of my own marriage. Soon after, I had a new found self-confidence and was something of "a rebel with a cause." I could no longer let myself be manipulated and was slowly breaking the chains that held me captive for too long. I picked myself up by my bootstraps and worked hard to support my son and myself. I came to the realization that it would just be the two of us, forever, and that there was nothing wrong with that. I needed to be happy without a man and continue to "find" myself. I was finally quite content.

The one man left in my life was my brother and I adored him. He was a "nerd" growing up with his nose always stuck in a book. Well, this nerd went to Cornell at sixteen years old. He was accepted at Howard Medical School after only three years at Cornell because his MCAT scores were so high. He was published at twenty-five years old. He was one of the best Nephrologists in the United States, but, he was also one of the most down to earth "successful" people you could ever meet. (Yes ladies, as of this writing he is still single!)

I keep telling myself to remember the subdued, happy times and try to

sleep, sleep, sleep…

Tuesday September 5th

Ronnie slept well. I slept fitfully; tossing and turning as the whirlwinds continually interrupted what little rest I tried to get. We got up at seven a.m. One of my main concerns and another reason I didn't sleep well was that I kept thinking about the air conditioner (installed above my side of the bed) in our bedroom. I had this gut feeling it wouldn't stay in the wall. I asked Ronnie to see about securing it before we lost electricity, since he might need power tools. After an hour of deep contemplation he couldn't come up with any solution. The wind was blustering and my stomach was in knots. We tried to keep occupied so we put our glass tabletops in the closets and shifted furniture here and there. At ten o'clock the electricity was shut off by the electric company, for safety reasons. Now it was pouring rain and the wind was gusting. It reminded me of the scene in the Wizard of Oz before the house started twirling up in the air. It seemed as though there was wind and rain hitting all sides of the house at one time. My head kept jerking from one spot to another as the sounds moved. I looked like Tippy Hendron in the Hitchcock movie "The Birds" when the house was being attacked.

We heard a splintering crack come from outside the kitchen door. Our Mango tree was the first casualty. I ventured close enough to peek out of the door and the winds seemed exceptionally strong to me. Ronnie said, "Oh, this is nothing." I was thinking if this was nothing, I didn't even want to try to imagine what "something" was ahead.

Our housekeeper, Adrienne and her husband, Derosi, lived in a small house behind ours. We used to use the house for storage. About a year earlier, immigration was picking up people that did not have the proper papers to be on the island. They were from Haiti and were "illegal" so we had them take refuge with us. We told them to come over to our house whenever they were "ready" ("ready" meaning scared enough) since we all thought our home was more secure and sturdy.

It was eleven o'clock in the morning and I started with (you guessed it) a glass of white wine, Adrienne had white wine too, Derosi had a cognac with coke and my husband had an O'Doul's non-alcoholic beer. (He stopped drinking five months ago, better him than me!) Now, let me set the backdrop: I had PMS, in a boarded up house, with three dogs, three other adults and a ten-year-old child during a seriously major hurricane. Stop laughing. Do you remember the shower scene in Psycho? I could visualize this becoming my reality, so besides the wine bottle I hit the Midol bottle too!

P.S. Remember ladies, when you are about to be in a storm associated with water there are a couple of "to do" tips they don't tell you about:

1. Buy tampons covered with an outer plastic wrapper and that have plastic applicators, the paper ones don't hold up very well!

2. Put all sanitary napkins and panty shields in a secure plastic bag to keep dry, there is nothing worse than a "pre" soggy sanitary napkin!! (Guys I apologize for the graphics but this has to be made known.)

The sounds surrounding us were indescribable. Things were clanging, knocking and thumping. The wind was howling, blowing and screeching. This was just the beginning…

One o'clock: the dogs looked as though they were saying, "what the hell is going on out there!" I looked like a deer with two headlights shining in its face. Shari was calm, cool and collected. She was looking at me like I was crazy for being nervous at that point. Oh, to be a child! Ronnie was constantly moving, keeping busy. What he was doing I truly didn't have a clue, but it was working for him. The radio signal was still on and that succeeded in drowning out the litany of clashes somewhat.

We proceeded to play a card game of gin, starving for a distraction of any kind. My hands were shaking badly and the sensation in my stomach was like a tug of war was going on. I checked the time, it was moving more slowly than a snail in quicksand. I gave up looking at the clock, I took it down, it was too much torture.

Ronnie suggested that I go lie down in the bedroom and try to take a nap. I said, "No way am I going in that bedroom. I know that the air conditioner is coming out of the wall. The winds are worse and I don't trust it, I'll just stay here in the kitchen for now." Let me describe this air conditioning unit. It was a twenty four thousand BTU air conditioner, really a commercial sized unit, suitable for use in hotel rooms. It took two to three men just to install it in the wall. Sure enough, the guys heard a loud noise and rushed to the kitchen door to look for the origin. Invisible marionette strings pulled me to the bedroom door and I looked in. The air conditioner was not in the wall! There was just a gaping hole. I ventured in further and saw it on the floor on the opposite side of the room.

"Ronnie. Ronnie, the air conditioner blew out of the wall," I screamed. He came running over and once he saw the hole he said "Holy shit," his face showed disbelief. "It looks like it blew in, bounced on the bed and continued across the room," he said. We gave each other a knowing look since no words were necessary. If I had been in that bed I would have been seriously injured or dead. The men scrambled for some of the wood they brought in earlier for just such an emergency. The wind continued to pound the cement wall surrounding the hole. It proceeded to buckle around the remaining window frame and cracked as easily as glass. I prayed that the entire wall did not follow. Trying to hammer a nail into our cement walls was nearly impossible without a high-speed drill, because of how they were made. (I don't know how Ronnie did it manually, but I am reminded of the shows that you see on television where people gain super strength in emergency situations.) On the opposite side of the room were mirrored glass closet doors. I asked Ronnie to take them down in case the temporary covering over the hole gave out, allowing any flying objects to smash into them. Since I had some new clothes in those closets he advised me to put them in plastic garbage bags to save them from possible water damage.

While awaiting the next possible emergency my husband cooked dinner, baked chicken and rice. The kitchen window above the sink was taped but not boarded up. I implored Ronnie to put more tape on it, especially because he was standing directly in front of it. He didn't feel it was necessary but did it anyway to appease me. He had to force me to eat some food. No one else needed encouragement.

My tolerance level was not stabilizing so my husband decided it was time to move me up to the hard stuff. He produced a potent cognac and coke. Those kept appearing miraculously, one after another. I could only assume he wanted me to pass out so as not to be coherent much longer (or alleviate me from driving him more crazy *or* perhaps he glimpsed that "psycho" look earlier!). Before we lost the radio signal, we got the location of the hurricane and one of the last coordinates was 18 degrees. We were about 18.2 degrees.

Time was in an abeyance. Twilight Zone episodes flickered in and out of my light stupor. You know the ones, where people found themselves in places that seemed surreal? They knew that the places must be some kind of bad dream because they were just too far fetched!

In the Caribbean most of the roofs are made of wood. Then, to keep the elements out, the wood is covered over with sheets of metal called "zinc". The zinc was either secured down with nails or screws. The most secure houses had roofs made of cement. There were not many that had cement roofs because it was very, very expensive to make them.

I kept replaying in my mind a radio call that I had heard during Hurricane Hugo, a few years ago. A woman was on the phone as she stood in her house, in the rain; her roof had already been ripped off by the winds. She was making a plea for help and the radio personality was advising her to go into the bathtub, closet or kitchen cabinet for cover. That telephone call wrenched everyone's heart that heard it. Would we now be meeting this same fate? First, I prayed that we could escape unharmed when these winds from hell stopped. Secondly, I prayed for the roof not to give in to the magnetism of the gusts and leave us completely exposed.

I kept picturing my son, Jeffrey, fifteen years old. He was currently living in New York, with his father. Ronnie's fifteen-year-old son, Ron Jr., lived with his mother in Arkansas. I loved them so much and my heart was aching with wonder. Would I ever see them again? Would I be around to share their experiences, give advice, know the men they would become? We had all just spent a great summer here together. Would there be another one?

I used to wonder what people would contemplate not knowing if they would survive or not. For us there was just too much time. My mind ran the gambit.

Great, I moved here to die! How did I get here? Oh yeah, that fateful weekend in New York…

1987

I had been separated for three years, my mother had passed away in 1986 and I purchased the house where I grew up. Ironically enough, my best friend Michelle (who lived next door to me when we were growing up) bought her mother's house and we were neighbors again. Déjà vu. Now, we had our own children. Michelle was remarried and now had three children: Chris, Danielle and Dominique. Michelle and I rode to work together on the subway, spoke on the phone twice during the day and returned home together. That not being enough, we were back and forth to each other's house several times each evening. I sensed that both of us were driving her husband, Kenny, crazy. He felt like the two of us were married and that I spent more time than he did with his own wife. Our bond was too close, we couldn't be deterred, and we were closer than most sisters were.

Suddenly, out of the blue, I got a call from Ronnie, who had moved to St. Maarten several years ago. He explained that since my brother had moved he didn't have his new phone number, so I gave it to him. He proceeded to tell me he had to come to New York to renew his passport. "Well, stop by and say hello. I haven't seen you in about seven years." "I'll try," he responded.

One Saturday, I was busy painting and making repairs on my house. His possible visit was already forgotten. While I was trying to spackle some holes in a wall left from removed bookshelves, the doorbell rang. I went to the door and it was Ronnie. "Ronnie, Ronnie" I yelled excitedly, as we hugged like long lost friends do. Eventually, we stepped back and took good long looks at each other. Hello! He looked very, very good and sexy! Chocolate brown skin, short wavy black hair, thick mustache (Billy Dee Williams is a point of reference for the looks and Richard Pryor for the sense of humor!). We reminisced for hours, rehashing old times, both good and bad. I could sense myself start to shift away from those old "like a brother" feelings. My uncle was there and asked Ronnie if he thought he would ever remarry. He responded, "Yes, if I find the right woman." I very nonchalantly raised my hand to volunteer. Subtle, very subtle. Ronnie caught this but did not respond, he just smiled. We ended up talking for six hours and I didn't want him to leave. Unfortunately, he had made plans already, a date with someone else! He said he would try to stop by again tomorrow.

I could not get him out of my mind. I felt like a schoolgirl, silly. After being such good friends for so long it was very strange to now think of him romantically. This was ridiculous I tried to convince myself. Get a grip, you grew up with him and he never felt that way toward you.

On Sunday the anticipation was killing me. Time was going as slow as Heinz ketchup pours. I was getting nervous. "What if he didn't come back." "Did I scare him off"? I said to myself. Finally, at five o'clock the doorbell rang. I was ecstatic to see him and the huge smile on my face was a dead give away. He was beaming and seemed as nervous as a hooker in church! We were both acting giddy and talked again for six hours. (Later we realized that we wanted to confess to each other the change in our feelings, but were both scared of rejection.) "You and I" by Black Ivory was playing in the background and this was putting me over the edge. How much could one take? Step one, after a few vodka and grapefruits Ronnie said "I don't know how you will react, but I'd really like to kiss you." I was thinking "Thank God", but said "That's fine with me." We looked like two porcupines trying to fit together! If it had been anyone else we would have known how to kiss. You would have thought we were retarded, it was hysterical. Step two, to the bedroom. Oh, don't try that "so soon" tone with me. I had known him for over twenty years. The kiss was awkward enough, the bedroom scene turned into animation. You could cut the tension with a knife, maybe a machete. It was many, many moons ago since we had played doctor. Someone had to break the ice so I said, "my, how you have grown!" That pretty much did it, we both collapsed in laughter. After that the ice surely melted. He proposed that same night and I said yes. We hadn't seen each other in seven years and now two days later, we were engaged. Needless to say, friends and family were shocked, but happy for us.

Ronnie's main concern was that he did not want to move back to New York. I said, "You have sun, sand and water.

I'm there." My employer and coworkers thought I was a raving lunatic when I went into work on Monday with my news. "We didn't even know you were seeing someone." "I wasn't," I replied. I then proceeded to bring them up to speed. People can be so funny. Why is it if it were them moving to the Caribbean it would be great, but me, I must be insane? Well, too bad.

My fairy tale was beginning…

Meanwhile, back at the hurricane…

In the wake of the air conditioner incident I believed that the next safest spot was in an alcove where my office was situated. (Ronnie was a liquor salesman, I was his "sexatary" and worked out of my home.) Shari settled under my desk and laid down on pillows from the couch. She had a flashlight, was reading a book and was still remarkably calm. I took up quarters in the chair next to her. Lucy, the "Dobie" joined us and cuddled in Shari's lap, like a baby. I plunged into a book myself, hell bent on any diversion, if only for a brief time. Adrienne and Derosi stayed on the couch, there wasn't enough room for everyone.

I told Ronnie I should have purchased some Depends (adult pampers). I was constantly in fear so I had the sensation that I always had to pee, even though I didn't. I could definitely recommend this item on a hurricane checklist, people!

The winds were hammering us and you could actually feel the pressure build up and then get released through the openings we had left for this purpose, cross ventilation. Remember being in an airplane and your ears popped? Well, this was the amount of pressure we were experiencing, our ears were popping! I couldn't believe this and it was making me more aware of the true force of Mother Nature, lurking too close for comfort.

We could hear the galvanized zinc on the roof bending and straining to stay on. I was reminded of the torturous sounds of nails scratching a chalkboard. Could you conceive of listening to that for (I don't know how many) hours? I think not. It seemed as though there was a giant standing above the house just ripping off the protective covering, the same way you would open a pull-up can of pudding.

I don't remember the precise time it started raining in the house. Regardless, it was now leaking all over. The bedroom carpet was becoming saturated. Beds, furniture cushions, tables, and floors were wet. Now I understood why they were called "drop" ceilings! When they get wet they drop every which way. Ronnie had to spot me with an umbrella as I relieved myself, for fear of those ceiling parts landing on my head. Three quarters of my bathroom ceiling were down already and turning to mush in puddles of water. By the way, for the great minds that came up with the hurricane preparation lists - you should have told everyone that if they have drop ceilings above their tubs not to fill the tubs with water. All you get is ceiling porridge! "Water, water everywhere and not a drop to drink," kept playing in my mind. Slowly, water invaded our current domain. The ceiling above the alcove was also a drop ceiling. Fearing which part would come crashing down first, I arranged a big white pillow on top of my head. I looked like a deranged Pillsbury doughboy. How come Shari could look like a harem girl with all of the pillows underneath and around her?

After watching me for a short while Ronnie came over, pulled the rest of this drop ceiling down, and placed a shower curtain on the remaining wood frame to catch the incoming intrusion of water above us. We had to try to preserve this sanctuary we had come to trust. Then, we grabbed some plastic bags and covered my computer and printer. "The stereo too," I reminded him. We scrambled to save what we believed was still salvageable. We threw CD's, cassettes, and VCR tapes haphazardly in bags and at least being busy temporarily distracted us. Adrienne and Derosi were now holding umbrellas to try and stay dry.

The now cyclonic winds were whooshing, wheezing, whistling, and wailing. Unknown objects could be heard bending, cracking, hitting, and careening all around like in a circular theater with ultrasound blasting at an unnerving pitch. Ronnie described the experience this way: remember watching a scary movie and you couldn't take it anymore. You got up and walked out? Well, we were stuck, we couldn't leave and unfortunately we had the lead roles in this horror flick.

Minutes seemed like an eternity. We went from room to room to evaluate the amount of water that had accumulated thus far. Only one bed in our back (third) bedroom was still three quarters dry. Ronnie shifted furniture around and prepared a spot to lay Shari down to sleep. We kept her clothes and sneakers on; you never knew when a rapid escape might be necessary. She quickly succumbed to exhaustion and slept like a log, even amidst this mayhem. God, how I envied her.

Why did the melody from the Wizard of Oz continue to play in my head? You know the one: "The house began to pitch...," I couldn't recall the rest of it. At least that took ten minutes of my time, working on the lyrics.

Peace was evasive. Hour after hour the wind continued to test our endurance. I was beginning to believe that it was winning. I didn't think that the eternal tension all over my body could possibly persevere indefinitely. My feet felt like they were imbedded in cement and I couldn't move. I just wanted to relax my muscles, just lay down and relax.

I had never been more scared in my life or for my life and those around me. All of us were silently praying. I started crying, softly at first, then harder. The housekeeper joined in and the men rushed to our respective sides to provide what comfort they could. At least this seemed to have allowed a small, yet short-lived reprieve from the knots in my body. Ronnie was trying to be the rock for all of us, but intuitively I could tell he was scared. Someone had to be the captain of this ship (though we were taking on quite a bit of water) and oversee all of us scared rats looking like we were ready to bail from the ship. Lord knows though that Hurricane Luis the Energizer Bunny was alive and well outside, going and going and going and going.

Ronnie looked at me and could tell I was ready to be sick. He took me to the bathroom to purge myself of the (until then) soothing cognac and cokes.

My back had given up now along with a part of my spirit so I went to stretch out next to Shari. Sleep was elusive. I kept praying, to God, to my mother and to my mother-in-law: "Please, let this end soon and let us all be okay." There was a lull in the gusts, but it was treachery, just a tease. It was not easing but building back up. Ronnie explained to me that the lull was called the eye or center of the hurricane. Then, it seemed to smack you back to reality that it was not ready to end yet. In the beginning, the winds and rain came from one direction. After the eye, with it's calm, it shifted and the tail was now attacking us from the opposite direction. Ronnie eventually came in and laid down next to me. We talked briefly. "How much longer is this going to continue?" I asked. "I don't know, baby. I just don't know," he replied. I laid my head on his chest, feeling a bit better from the solace it provided. He put his arm around me and drew me closer. I was clinging to him like a babe to its mother for protection. More hours crawled by as I begged for daylight. The repetitiveness of a metronome might actually be welcome now. At the very least it would give you something else to concentrate on. Perchance, with the daylight, relief would come. Maybe then you could see where the sounds were coming from, without relying on your imagination. My patience was shot. I was scared to even contemplate what was transpiring outside of our home. Besides, wondering too much now was gnawing away at the tiny bit of energy I had left. These hours had been pure hell. Yet, my mind started wandering and I thought about others that I knew, personally, who had been through hard trials, for longer periods of time. Like my Great Uncle, Colonel Haldane King. He was one of the original Thirteen Tuskegee Airmen. I thought about the trials and tribulations of that era… He had to expend a hundred times the effort of a white pilot to be "accepted" and then not really. These people brazed insurmountable odds and prevailed. It gave me a renewed respect. Others might not make the correlation, might not learn anything from this disaster. It was truly their loss.

If we could endure the past twenty hours whereas others had endured years, there was a light at the end of the tunnel.

I lay there, waiting for our light to arrive…

Wednesday September 6th 7:00 AM

The rains and winds have not ceased, but they have eased. Ronnie told me it was lighter now, I was not convinced. He went out the kitchen door, the only easy access in or out. Soon I heard the boards (plywood) being taken down from the front sliding glass doors. I surveyed the living room and kitchen. One candle was still burning, undaunted by all the wind and water. It once belonged to my mother. I was reminded once again that she still watched over me. "Thanks mom!"

The front yard looked like we just installed a swimming pool, water was abundant. We lived at the bottom of the mountains so the water ran out of the hills and consequently rested by us. The water in front was deeper, measuring three to four feet, than on the sides of the house, about two feet.

Our car was in water up to the hood. Amazingly, our front windshield that had had a crack in it for the past year was still intact. Ronnie waded to the rear of the car. "The back windshield is broken out and there is a big dent in the right side," he yelled back. I just shrugged, thinking, "who cares?"

The dogs took out after him, happy to be free again themselves. Plus, they liked to play in muddy water so they were happy as pigs in a pen. A small portion of our front gate was left but the balance of it was nowhere in sight. Our once gorgeous Flamboyant tree had been stripped naked. The Palm tree next to it was decapitated. Zinc was everywhere. When I said everywhere, I meant everywhere. Some pieces were bent so badly that they could be used as (ugly) sculptured art. The trees that I could see for a couple of blocks away were barren, if still standing at all. Our gutters were also nowhere to be found. In the back yard we had a new "zinc" tree house.

Still nervous about the continually blowing winds I went back inside to make some tea. Water was in every item that would hold it. I didn't even attempt to clean at that point. Thank goodness we could still use the stove since it was hooked up to a gas bottle. I put drinking water on to boil. I made Ronnie a cup of coffee, while I fixed a (go ahead and make a guess, no it's too early for that!) hot tea with cognac and of course Sweet and Low! Little did I know that this would become my morning ritual for the next few days.

I didn't know where Ronnie was or what he was doing. I went into the second bathroom, not totally flooded (only an inch of water instead of two to three). I took a wrought-iron porch chair to sit on, at least this was easily dried. Eventually he found me and reassured me that it was okay to come out now. I stood on the front porch while the now tamed but incessant winds whipped around me. There was a raging stream running through the street. Before long people started appearing on the street, we lived on a main road. Shortly thereafter jeeps were driving past. The curious and adventurous were out early to examine what exactly had transpired during the day and night of hell.

Our housekeeper and her husband set off to examine their dwelling. It was fine. The whole roof was intact and it was dry inside. So much for believing our place was more secure! We finally realized that this was probably because buildings that were taller surrounded their house on all sides and therefore protected it.

The tenants came sloshing over through the new "Samuels Bay." They looked like tight ropewalkers with their arms outstretched and performing balancing acts. The water was so deep and muddy you couldn't see where to step and what was stable, there was zinc, nails and wood submerged. If you fell you might be badly cut. They had lost all of the zinc plus half of the wood from their roof. They told us they spent the last five hours in the bathroom under a mattress with four adults, two children (four and two years old) and two dogs. I had the notion that we had it so bad. All of the zinc had been ripped off of our roof, too. Our roof was leaking all over, but we still had the wood over our heads. Our place, though soaked, was still dryer than theirs was. I never knew that there could be degrees of saturation! They asked if they could all come over. We said, "sure no problem". They went back to gather some belongings while I brewed another pot of water for coffee and hot chocolate. Shari, having come out of her coma, was ready for breakfast. I told her that I had to quickly use up the balance of the milk, so I fixed her corn flakes.

I began sweeping water out the front and side doors but it was a losing battle. My next brilliant idea was to strategically place pots and pans to retrieve the ever-dripping water. The house looked like a cartoon scene. Then, I started searching for dry clothes for the neighbors to change into, luckily I still had some. The water had not yet invaded the towels and linens, closets or dressers.

I put the patio table in one spot that was not being trickled on (so far as I could tell), so everyone could sit and endeavor to stay dry. After getting everyone settled I beat a hasty retreat to the front porch. It was not that I was being unsociable. I was still suffering from PMS and I didn't need to be inside with five dogs, five adults and two "little ones" if I didn't have to! Shari joined me, feeling the same way. I picked my book up where I left off yesterday.

Ronnie waded out to the car again and pushed it to shallow water. He was able to start it, he shouted "Yes, Yes!" like someone who had just scored a touchdown.

The next scene, at ten in the morning, was quite intriguing. People were walking with bags, shopping carts and suitcases. They appeared to be laden with groceries and sundries. Ronnie spoke to a passerby. It seemed that one of the larger supermarkets was badly damaged. There was a colossal "Supermarket Sweep" with hundreds of participants. Not to condone anyone's actions but for many it was a case of pure survival. Self-preservation, the first law of nature, overtook their minds. Hundreds were homeless, penniless, desperate and had families to provide with food and the basic necessities. The supermarket owners knew that thousands of items would only be thrown out anyway, unable to be sold.

Ronnie attempted to check on Shari's Grandmother, she lived up the road from us. He returned a brief while later because he was unable to pass by car. He took off on foot. In an hour he arrived back home. She was fine, her house was in one piece, still dry and they had a generator. We agreed to take Shari to stay there. "We are so lucky. We are so lucky," was all he could verbalize. He said he saw some houses totally destroyed, nothing, a pile of rubble. Many places were now roofless and having had their contents sucked out, looked like dollhouses.

Ronnie decided to go view his company's warehouse, a ten-minute drive away. He got back two hours later (he had also gone to see one of the managers to advise him of the situation.) "I don't know if I have a job," he said. "The warehouse was half-demolished." Nothing phased me at this point. We were all alive. Anything above and beyond that was a bonus. It's funny how your total outlook on life can change. That is not to say that I was materialistic before this. You just have a serenity that all will be alright because you are alive. Things can be rebuilt and replaced, you cannot. There was no time to dwell on it now anyway, there were numerous tasks to do. He took off again to locate family members and ensure that they were uninjured.

I contemplated what to prepare for dinner for this huge clan. How about trying something new and different? NOT! Chicken and rice again it was. I needed to use up the food that would spoil the quickest anyway instead of throwing it out. I served it up on fine plastic china. I was so thankful that we were still able to cook. Life's simple pleasures…

I didn't know where the day went. Nighttime had arrived already. The kids were beat. We set out to make sleeping arrangements. The wet sheets were stripped off and the sopping mattresses were covered with plastic. Next, we placed a layer of towels so everyone didn't sweat to death, topped off with clean sheets. The pillows were unusable. Folded towels placed in pillowcases served as a substitute. Improvisation would be the word for days to come. There were still a couple of inches of water on the floors so you needed a towel close by to dry your feet before you got into bed.

The skies were quiet and the rain had subsided allowing us time to replenish our zapped energies. Mosquito coils were lit for further comfort. When there was water around, mosquitoes were plentiful. No one wanted to be kept awake by mosquitoes buzzing in their ears. We all passed out by ten o'clock.

Thursday September 7th 5:00 AM

The rain seemed to restrain itself for as long as possible, but it started again. It really wasn't easy to sleep with water splattering on your face. Welcome back to the olden days, we went to dip water from the cistern (a well under the house) to wash up with. By six-thirty all the troops were up. After morning coffee and tea Ronnie decided to take me on a sightseeing tour of the island. The destruction was unimaginable. Parts of houses were strewn about. Power lines were down with selected poles torn from their previous locations. Trees were uprooted and the zinc lying about seemed to be the new decor, as if chosen by all. There were half of some houses left, three quarters of others, none of some.

We saw homeowners as they searched through rubble to try to find items that could possibly be salvaged. The "Shanty Towns" (scantily built shacks clustered together) looked as if a giant had stepped on them. We drove on over the hill toward Simpson Bay. Unbelievably, as we passed through Cole Bay it appeared as before. You couldn't imagine a hurricane had caused so much destruction elsewhere on the island. In Simpson Bay however, boats and yachts had been tossed about like kiddy toys in a bathtub. They were resting precariously against buildings, on shore and on top of each other. They lined the Airport Road as if they were placed there on purpose. Masts were leaning over the road like half crossed swords at a military wedding. There was damage evident, but the destruction still didn't seem as bad as on our side of the hill. We turned around at the airport to head back so Ronnie could show me his company's warehouse in Point Blanche.

Enroute, we saw that the Electric Company (GEBE) office was in pieces and Landsradio (the Telephone Company) seemed to have thrown up its insides, they were strewn all about. We arrived at the warehouse. It was a shell of its former self. It was weird to see steel beams twisted like bobby pins, metal doors peeled back like bananas. We continued on through Madame Estates. The Food Fair Supermarket was unrecognizable, more than three-quarters of it were gone.

Fellow survivors told us we sustained winds with gusts of up to two hundred and thirty miles per hour. It surely made you realize the tremendous strength of Mother Nature and how truly blessed we were to be alive.

While driving back to our house pedestrians pointed out that we had two flat tires. Two, not one, two. Great. A light bulb went off in Ronnie's head. Shari's grandmother had the same type of car as ours. It was badly damaged and undrivable. Thankfully, she gave the tires to us. Finally, we arrived back home. The female tenants were in their house cleaning so they could sleep there tonight. The men were on their roof securing the plywood they had previously taken down from their windows. Hopefully, this temporary coverage on the roof would be able to protect them from the elements. The phrase "having a roof over your head" had taken on a new meaning for me. I came to realize what an integral part of the house this was. But if you thought about it, when did you really ever think about the roof? Ronnie explained that this was the reason that Caribbean people had such big parties once the roof was completed when building their homes.

Friends and family continuously drove by to make sure that we were unhurt. Meanwhile, clean up was the task slated for today and days to come. Adrienne miraculously reappeared to help. We were all working independently, yet together. No one was speaking. We were lost in our own private thoughts.

Bed time. I took a cat bath while Ronnie poured buckets of water over himself outside. The tub/shower was still filled with the drop ceiling porridge. We lit mosquito coils again, sprayed mosquito repellent all over ourselves and retired for the night. It started to rain. Ronnie went and got some plastic tarp and his staple gun and attached it to the wood ceiling above our bed. He was determined to sleep "rainfall free".

Friday September 8th 7:00 AM

Cleaning and drying. Drying and cleaning. Next, I started throwing out things that were unsalvageable and items that survived were placed in plastic bags. The silverware drawer had fallen apart so I stuck the plastic tray in the microwave. What? At least it will stay dry in there! If I just left it on the counter and it rained again it would be filled with water, again. Then, I put the furniture cushions, bed pillows, and mattresses out in the sun. We desperately implored them to get dry. This appeared to be being done by many all over the island.

Early in the afternoon we took a quick lunch break. A cold drink would sure feel good right now. Bingo! I remembered that a good friend of mine, Linda Papazian, was stuck on the island as a result of the hurricane. Her hotel had electricity because it was on the same line as the hospital. So, I went over with all of the two inch deep rectangular Tupperware I could find. Until she was able to leave the Island I could make ice. This was a very rare commodity. How refreshing it would be to have a cold drink while working so hard all day. (Actually, I confess I wanted the ice for my wine - who likes hot white wine? I'm only kidding. Or am I?)

Linda, along with many other tourists, was busy helping and assisting with daily hotel operations. Many vacationing people need to be acknowledged for their efforts during this terrible time of need on our island. They could have sat back and complained, some did, but most were happy to help. Thank you. Applause, applause.

Ronnie a.k.a. McGuyver, was busy developing inventions to try to make rural life just a little easier. The first device was a pulley system above the cistern opening.

He explained that his back was killing him from bending down to draw buckets of water plus he almost fell in last night! I apologized to him for laughing hysterically at the thought.

Our other problem was showering. He took a large cooler that we were not using, placed it next to the tub, and filled it with cistern water. Yes, I had cleaned up the ceiling porridge. He brought in some empty one liter drinking water bottles and filled them up. We took turns standing in the shower while pouring water over each other as we soaped up and rinsed off. Trust me, after working fifteen hours today we were grateful for this cold water cleansing. Hot water was a distant memory and we didn't know when we would get it again. Thank goodness I had naturally curly hair and didn't have to rely on a blow dryer or hot curlers.

For dinner we feasted on canned corned beef and rice. Then we passed out. Exhaustion was our entertainment those evenings.

Saturday September 9th 7:00 AM

It was so stifling without having fans on at night that the wait for daylight seemed endless. Today we had to rip the carpet up in our bedroom. It was starting to smell. Ronnie had to cut it up into small pieces for ease in handling because it was so heavy. Having lost its sponge the water rushed back to the floor. After sweeping the water from one room to another to get it outside I started to feel weak. I remembered that I had a dustpan with a long handle. I located that and a pail and walla! All I had to do was sweep the water into the dustpan and dump it in the pail. I didn't even have to bend over. My back was forever grateful.

Early in the afternoon we took a much-needed break. We cruised over to see Ronnie's Uncle on the French side of the Island. He was fine. No human casualties, yet he had lost a few head of cattle. He stocked bags of coals so we confiscated one. We never knew when the gas in the stove would finish and we could always barbecue!

Our next stop was the Cloud Room Restaurant, owned by Ronnie's cousin, Conrad. It used to be situated on a look out point above Orient Beach. Eighty percent of it was gone! The living quarters were spared and he was unharmed. Conrad said, "It sounded like twenty freight trains were driving through here. I thought it was never going to end." If no other stories were told, all survivors would repeat this comment over and over and over. The hurricane seemed endless.

We could look down at Orient Beach. There was not much left in the way of buildings and facilities. It looked like it did six years ago. Mother Nature reclaimed it.

Back home again, I emptied out our large freezer and cleaned the refrigerator. All of the meat had to be burned. It was no longer edible. We couldn't take the chance of attracting bugs or rodents by just placing it raw in the garbage. Not to mention how that would smell. Lord knows when the garbage pick-up would start again.

There was a curfew from six at night to six in the morning. Where was there to go anyway? Besides, every inch of bone and muscle in my body was hurting and aching. We had never worked so hard and we were normally hard working people. Ronnie had blisters on his hands and feet. I had them on my hands. He said, "when was the last time you felt like this?" "Never. Never ever before in my life," I replied exhaustedly.

The closest I could remember on the exhaustion scale might have been after the Sinbad 70's Soul Music Festival…

May 24-29th, 1995

We were eagerly anticipating the Music Festival. We knew there would be quite a variety of groups participating, playing the music we grew up with. The acts coming were: The Average White Band, Confunkshun, Earth, Wind & Fire, Gladys Knight, Teena Marie, Frankie Beverly and Maze, The O'Jays, The Ohio Players, Rose Royce and War. Funky line-up wasn't it? Since live concerts like this were rarely held on St. Maarten, this was a treat indeed.

We were used to this when we were growing up in Queens. James Brown would hand out singles (45RPM) copies of his current hits and buttons that read "Say it Loud, I'm Black and I'm Proud". The Delfonics, Black Ivory, Blue Magic, Harold Melvin and the Blue Notes, The Dramatics and the Fat Back Band played often in our local theaters. We were very fortunate indeed while growing up.

My brother flew in from California, as well as some of his friends, to experience this virgin extravaganza on St. Maarten. Attending an initial pre-show, however, it would just be the three of us.

Rose Royce was performing at a free concert on Thursday being held at the La Belle Creole Hotel. What great memories came flooding back! Their song "Ooh Boy" I played repeatedly as a teenager, while I sang in front of the mirror. I can't believe all the words came back to my mind so easily, it had been quite a few years. The show was fantastic, excellent. Ronnie, providing the side show by dancing the old time "group" steps and singing to me, wasn't too bad either!

The main shows were to be held on Friday, Saturday and Sunday nights, with beach parties held during the day. The show would air as if it had been filmed continuously in one night. Some locals said that they would just watch the

Special on HBO. It would be the same thing. Wrong! First of all there was nothing like a live concert and second, a great deal would be left on the editing room floor.

Ronnie and I had agreed not to work during this time, to enjoy this once in a lifetime experience to the maximum. My brother caught up with his friends and was hanging out with them. Ronnie and I had our game plan set already so we decided to "see 'em when we see 'em!"

The concerts were slated to start at eight o'clock in the evening but we were in line at four o'clock! Recalling New York concerts, we knew that the tourists from the United States would be vying for their "spots". There weren't any seats. We would be standing on the stadium grounds. The partying would start while we were in line. Everyone was friendly, conversing and laughing. One couple in particular we had a fun time with every night. They were wearing Afro wigs. We nicknamed them Angela (Davis) and Don

(Cornelius), real names: Darcell and George McCoy. The next character we named "Bucket" because she always brought along a bucket to sit on. My husband, the biggest ham and one of the funniest characters cast during this "preview", was nicknamed "Spicy". That came from the spicy way his stories were told!

Once inside the stadium we would all get started dancing. The engineers were playing tapes of old school music and we danced the bump, the tighten-up and sang while waiting for the live show to begin. We would continue dancing for hours through the shows, so our legs felt like putty by the end of each night.

Finally, the HBO Special aired and what to my wandering eyes should appear but Kim and Ron, shown here and there! We were in shock. We must have been on screen about four times (really more but only because we were looking specifically for ourselves!) Everywhere we went in St. Maarten all we heard was "HBO, HBO. We saw you on HBO. How did you get shown so much? Who did you know?" We were now local celebrities. (Maybe because we wore the same color shirts each night and this was supposed to appear as if it was filmed in one night. It looked like we were wearing the same clothing, so we were shown more.) Anyway, we would like to thank Sinbad for this highlight in our lives. It was a memory we wouldn't soon forget!

Forget, forget, forget....

Sunday September 10th 4:30 AM

I couldn't sleep. The trauma finally surfaced. I was too preoccupied before, dealing with the clean up chores. Tears slowly slid down my face. I was powerless to hold them back any longer. I remembered all of the turmoil we had just lived through. My body began shaking and I started to cry uncontrollably. At least crying helped to release some of the tension. I started to take deep breaths and reminded myself that it was over. Again, I thanked God for being with us.

Ronnie got up at six-thirty. We plunged into yet another repetitive day of cleaning. All electrical items and appliances were put in plastic and secured in closets. We didn't know if they worked and we couldn't check them until the electricity was reconnected. We figured that wouldn't happen for a few more months. Besides, in the meantime, when it rained outside it also rained inside. So, to be on the safe side, things were getting "plasticized!"

Since our front gate vanished "McGuyver" set out to make a new one. We didn't want the dogs venturing out because a car could hit them. I was truly amazed at times at my husband's resourcefulness. He made a temporary gate in two hours. Thank God he was mine!

Fatigue ever present, we spent a relaxing night playing cards on the front porch, by candlelight.

Monday September 11th 7:00 AM

We were on the road. We decided to attempt to contact our family in the United States. Rumors were that there was phone service on the French side of the Island. We would prefer not to wait in long lines, hence the reason for starting early. Cellular phone service on the Dutch side had been reinstated. We had a cell phone. But you "kinda" needed electricity to charge the batteries, catch twenty-two (no, we didn't have a car charger!). In Marigot two phones were free and we were able to contact Ronnie's parents. His mother started crying when she heard his voice. She had been able to get through to some other family members and was told that we were alright, but it was not the same as speaking with us directly. Family and friends in the states were going through their own kind of hell with worry and uncertainty as to what had transpired here on the island. Mom told us that a friend of hers, residing on St. Maarten, was interviewed on CNN. He was standing in the shell of his former house, all of the contents had been sucked out. He lived diagonally across the street from us! It was spooky. It seemed that there was a great deal of tornado action involved during the hurricane too. We told her to call our sons, since we were not sure if we could get through to them. Next, I contacted my brother, Keith, to advise him of our status. He too was relieved.

Ronnie's boss, Steve, lived not far out of the way from where the phones were located so we shot over there to see him. We were unsure of the status of the company's future. We were totally in the dark, no one had been by to advise us. Thankfully, he said the company would not pull out, but rebuild. Hallelujah!! A deep sigh of relief escaped from my lips. Ronnie's shoulders rose and fell in answer to the lifting of his own burden. Unemployment was reaching epic proportions following this disaster. Once again, we were among the lucky ones. Thank you Jesus! Thank you mommy!

Ronnie's boss relayed his hurricane experience. He stayed with someone else and not in his own house (his own house ended up having only minor damage.) The windows exploded out of the house where he was staying. Walls fell in as they escaped from room to room in fear of their lives. He said it was like a bad movie. Sound familiar? There were hundreds of movies played out that night, simultaneously. Steve and Ronnie agreed. If anyone said they were not scared, they were lying.

Home again, I came to grips with the fact that half of the clothes in my closet were too small for me. It was time to give up the fantasy that I would fit into them "someday". They had been hanging there for three years or more. I bagged up the clothes for those that could use and needed them, now. I gave my housekeeper two bags to distribute to her friends and took two bags to the Red Cross. I felt better by doing something to help others. While I was driving to the Red Cross I put the airco (air-conditioning for non-islanders) on in the car. That felt so good. Finally I felt a cool breeze, however temporary. Don't tell my husband! The gas lines were horrendous and he didn't want me to burn too much gas. I couldn't help it. O.K. tell him. I could always plead temporary insanity.

We ate corned beef for dinner. I am being very truthful when I say that I don't care to see this delicacy for quite awhile! My next book project should be "How Many Ways to Prepare Corned Beef." All of you guinea pigs that want to experiment and have suggestions, please feel free to submit them. I won't however, be tasting them. Thank you very much.

Tuesday September 12th

There was an employee meeting at the warehouse scheduled for ten o'clock that morning. We both went. One of the managers was standing under a precariously situated air-conditioner and someone made a comment that he should not stand there because it could dislodge and plummet onto his head. He, however, had grown up in construction and said not to worry it seemed stable enough. Ronnie said, "There are many people that grew up in construction and have been killed. The building was then dedicated to them!" Game plans were organized for clean-up and temporary security, a priority, was set up.

We returned home so Ronnie could "hit the roof!" He was armed with tar, plastic, nails etc., and most importantly music. Musical accompaniment canceled out the monotony.

I could barely hold back the excitement of my next impending assignment. I got to peel the tape off of the windows. "Oh, joy. Could it get any better than this?" (To get the full impact of this statement it has to be read like Betty Davis when she said, "What a dump!")

The water in our yard had finally rescinded. It was so nice to have dry feet again. Every time you left the house (after it was finally dry inside) you would have to walk through water to get to the car. Then you would have to carry an extra pair of shoes and a towel to dry off your feet once inside the car. I felt like a duck, with perpetually wet feet. Socks and sneakers had been constantly rotated in shifts for drying.

That night we sat on the porch, played cards by candlelight again and listened to relaxing music (no rap right now, thanks anyway). The sound of a backhoe could be heard close by. They were cleaning out the guts

(Caribbean word for the drainage ditches on the side of the road). Ronnie collected the zinc and wood from our yard and tossed it over the wall, into our gut, to be disposed of. Accidentally, a nail caught his hip, ripping through clothes and flesh. He wouldn't show me. "It's not real deep," he said. Knowingly, he went to the hospital. Even if stitches were not needed a tetanus shot couldn't hurt. (As it turned out they had been inundated with many such injuries.) This served to appease me. We definitely didn't need extra things to worry about.

Wednesday September 13th

All was quiet. We decided to go by a few of Ronnie's accounts to find out if they were going to reopen and/or when. We listened to new hurricane adventure stories. There was no shortage of these, believe me. Everyone was eager to rehash their experiences, which seemed to help get over the trauma.

Cars, jeeps, trucks and vans. I would approximate that every two out of four we passed had at least one window missing somewhere. Many had dents from flying debris or falling trees. Various colors of plastic adorned them and appeared to be the norm. It's strange how your eyes adjust to the signs of destruction still visible. It seemed commonplace now.

Roof duty again for Ronnie. He was trying to put some type of sealant on the wood to keep it from getting totally ruined. After hours working in the searing sun he had a much deeper tan! He was dark skinned before, now, he was black. He said to me "If you really want a tan go up on the roof. You'll have one in ten minutes!"

The house was clean and dry, almost back to normal. The decor did seem rather sparse though with so many items out of sight. An enormous job well done. Satisfaction at last! We overcame the huge tasks set before us and conquered them all. So far, so good.

Someone told us that Sambuca Restaurant was open. Curfew or not we didn't care, we were getting antsy staying home. Plus they had food, real food, and no corned beef. When we got there they had chicken, beef, salads and more. Heaven. I was shocked to see so many people had gone against the curfew too! We caught up and mingled with friends we had been unable to see before then and big hugs were abundant. We had all gotten through the hurricane safely. Everyone had been working hard at cleaning up. It was great to be out and feel almost normal again.

Of course, this was too good to be true…

ROUND TWO

Thursday September 14th

I was relaxing, writing more on this story and listening to the radio. It was two o'clock in the afternoon. The following radio announcement was made: "All employers are requested to close at four o'clock to allow their employees time to go home and prepare for Hurricane Marilyn. It is approaching and will affect us in the early morning hours tomorrow." I was in total shock. I was paralyzed, petrified. I just stared at the radio. This couldn't be happening. I called Ronnie down from the roof and repeated what I had just heard. He looked like he was doped up, on drugs, spaced out. Our tenant came over to find out if

Hurricanes, Paradise and Fairy Tales

we had heard. Yes, we shook our heads. In unison, we all kept saying, "we can't take anymore, this is not happening."

GROUND HOG DAY!

Did you see that movie? It was extremely funny to those watching. If you were in Bill Murry's shoes it might not have seemed so… In the movie, he recalled a fantastic day that he had once. He was with a beautiful woman and they had fantastic sex for hours. Why couldn't he be living that day over and over and over again. No, he was getting Ground Hog Day reruns instead! I know a day that I would like repeated, my wedding day (to be specific, my second wedding)…

1988

I was watching Oprah one day and Dudley Moore was on. He said he had gotten married at "The Little Church of the West" in Las Vegas. Other celebrities were also mentioned that had nuptials performed there, too. There was an idea! Ronnie and I called Vegas and made arrangements to be married at that same church. (Ronnie had moved to Queens for 6 months to help me relocate to St. Maaerten.) For months I had been carrying around a picture of a wedding dress from Bridal Magazine that I wanted. I now had one week to find it. (Once we decided to go to Vegas we didn't want to wait). The third Bridal store we visited had it and in my size, unbelievable. You couldn't tell from the picture but it had a train and I didn't need all of that. They assured me they could make the alterations in time. I picked out the shoes and hat. I was set. Ronnie got his tuxedo rental, everything was falling neatly into place.

The airline stewardess treated us wonderfully (she saw the clothes we were carrying) and gave us complimentary champagne. We arrived in Vegas in the morning on July 6, 1988. The wedding was at four. At check in we told the front desk clerk our plans and she upgraded us to a junior suite! All of the employees we encountered were friendly, outgoing and always ready to help. I arranged for a maid to come to the room later to button up the back of my dress for me. Ronnie still hadn't seen it and I couldn't button it by myself. We took off to get the marriage license. This was really interesting. They didn't even ask us for any identification! You filled out a form, they asked you your mother's maiden name, you gave them the fee and you got the license. I was thinking "is this legal?" No wonder bigamy was so easy. Meanwhile, I tried to relax and decided to get a manicure. You know how you always think you have enough time for all of your pre-arranged plans? Yeah, well time was flying by and now I had to rush.

Ronnie got dressed and had to zoom off to the airport to pick up my brother. He will give me away and then switch over and be the best man. It would be just the three of us. He got back from the airport at about three forty-five. His eyes lit up when he saw me looking like the intended bride that I was. I'm sorry, I neglected to tell you how handsome he was looking. Gorgeous pretty much summed it up. We caused quite a stir as we went through the Flamingo Hotel. People were stopping and staring and told us how great we looked. A nice boost for the ego, let me tell you. We rushed and made it just in time for our appointment.

The Church was filled with all of our vampire friends and family (they didn't come out on tape because you can't photograph vampires!). Ronnie was so nervous I thought I could hear his knees knocking together.

The ceremony was quaint, not long, just enough. At one point the minister told Ronnie to give me his left hand and he gave me the right one. "The other left one," the minister corrected. I was trying not to crack up. It was a very lovely, simple occasion and the church was beautiful. We stopped, took pictures, and then went out to dinner, my brother's treat. We went to a restaurant where they cooked the food on the grill in front of you. Keith ordered Cristal to toast with. This was just fantastic. I had my two favorite guys with me, no big crowds of well wishers so that you couldn't really enjoy the day. After some more Cristal my brother said he had to get back to California to be at work in the morning. When he got the check his eyes opened a lot wider. "This is more than I have ever spent for dinner for three people. As a matter of fact this is more than I have spent for dinner for ten people!" Not that he was complaining, just stating a fact.

We dropped him off at the airport and rushed off to a comedy show we had made reservations for. There were so many people in line but Ronnie went up to the usher and slipped him a tip. Next thing I knew I was sitting with my elbow on the stage! The show was great. Next we decided to go to a disco. Now, I was still in my wedding dress (I planned on getting my moneys worth out of it) and the bouncer asked me for my identification. Hello! They didn't even ask me for my identification at the marriage bureau. I was old enough to get married but not go into the disco? Did he think someone under age would go to the trouble of wearing a wedding dress just to be able to get in? No, it must be that I just looked so young. Ronnie must have robbed the cradle. Ronnie was pissed off. "You want to see her ID. I bet she's older than you are." He took it out of his wallet (I didn't have any place to carry it). Yes, I was older than the guy carding me. Hell. I didn't care. I felt so good about him asking me to prove that I was eighteen and shocking Ronnie it was worth it! By the way, I was twenty-nine.

We got back to the hotel and ordered room service. It had to be four in the morning. The food was exceptional. The set up was extravagant. Again, everything was perfect.

Why can't we repeat that day?

Friday September 15th

At least in preparation for Marilyn I didn't have to cut the steel again. Ronnie retrieved the plywood and supplies to re-board up the windows while Shari and I re-taped the windows. (Ronnie had picked her up earlier today). Oh yes, you know my wine tasting had started too.

Being a seasoned "hurricane buster" now, I put everything I can see in plastic. Most of the household items had previously met this fate in the last week anyway. I reupholstered the now dry furniture, in plastic. Countertops, dressers and tables were once again bare. We were all working in a daze. The worst part was that the local news reports were very vague. We didn't know what to expect, so we prepared for another "Luis". Radio personalities jokingly said that if we got through Luis this would be a piece of cake. I was not laughing.

The evening was warm with a refreshing breeze. We sat outside, music penetrating the surrounding stillness. The roads were deserted. People were home, if they had one left, hunkering down. Shari was dancing around the porch while I read by flashlight. Ronnie occupied his mind playing with the dogs. Eventually, they both went to bed, but I stayed up and read. An hour later I retreated to the living room and stretched out on the couch. Ronnie woke me up at four o'clock in the morning. It had started. The rain was infiltrating the house. The same house that it took us a week, filled with blood, sweat, and tears, to get dry.

Candles were lit and the place had an eerie glow, it was not romantic. Shari and I sat at the table again, situated in the same non-drip spot as last week, between the kitchen and living room. Ronnie was in another room, I didn't know what he was doing (I don't seem to keep track of him too well, do I?) Shari nonchalantly said to me "I just saw a rat run behind the microwave on the kitchen counter." She was so calm that I said, "Are you sure it wasn't a big mouse?" "No. It was a rat," she assured me. She then proceeded to walk closer to the counter for a better look. I started talking like the Tin Man out the side of my mouth. "Shari, are you crazy? Come back over here and sit down," I pleaded. "It's just like a small cat," she quipped. I seriously think this child needs some therapy. Once she returned I couldn't keep my eyes off of the counter. I was waiting and staring, staring and waiting. Then, lo and behold I saw it! It was big and black, searching for a dry spot like the rest of us. Well, I am so sorry but I didn't feel very neighborly right then…

This was all I needed. No longer PMS but MS with three dogs, my husband, Shari and a rat for my second hurricane. I had to write this down, I didn't even believe it. Seasoned writers couldn't even dream up stuff like this. "Ronnie, Ronnie. Get in here now. There's a rat on the counter," I screamed. Normally, I would be standing on a chair if I saw a mouse, but I was frozen. I don't know if I thought that it would come after me or what. The louvered kitchen windows were still partially open and eventually he was able to shoo our houseguest out. Relief. Big time. Going back to school and taking exams is looking good right now. I don't know how many more of these tests I can take without having heart failure.

Forget the wine, I think this calls for a straight cognac, what do you think? All righty then. "Hey honey, don't be so stingy with the cognac." Might as well throw caution to the wind, so to speak!

Torrential rain. This was just what we, and all of St. Maarten, needed. Yes, I was being facetious. One way to verify the strength of the patchwork on the roof was with more rain. It was not passing its test either. Was it my imagination or was it raining more inside than out?

Drip. Drop. Drip. Drop. Drip. Drop. This movie sequel was set in a veritable dungeon. It was a feature film. The second of the series entitled "The Chinese Water Torture Chamber" starring, you guessed it - Ron and Kim Samuels. Yeeaah! The crowd roared.

I know that God will not burden you with more than you can bear, but we were getting awfully close here. I could see that infamous white jacket with the special straps as my new attire. Ronnie, I observed, was not far behind me. I watched him. I didn't say a word. "What the hell is he doing?", I asked myself. He was collecting candles from the whole house. His face showed intense concentration. He saw me raise my eyebrows questioningly. "I'm making a new candle from the melted wax," he explained. Okay, fine. He's lost it!

The dogs were busy scouting out a dry spot to lay down. Fat chance, I thought as I watched them. During the first hurricane we experienced the horrific winds and some rain. Now we had torrential rain and some wind. It was not a common occurrence to have a rainstorm throughout your house. My husband said furniture was described as a bedroom set or a kitchen set. The description does not include all weather. The furniture, therefore, was completely and utterly ruined. What Luis didn't wreck Marilyn finished off.

Luis blew me, Marilyn just got me wet!

Friday September 15th

Daylight, if you can call it that, came. Ronnie took the plywood off the sliding glass doors, for the second time. "Oh, our swimming pool is back, isn't that special!" The dogs went out to frolic in it, for the sixth time. I fixed a tea with cognac, for the tenth time. Then I started sweeping out water, for the fiftieth time.

I was sweeping and crying, crying and sweeping, and I lost it, whatever "it" was. I was hysterical, erupting like a volcano. "What am I a fish?" I yelled at no one in particular. "I can't take all this water anymore." "That's it. Stop it. Stop sweeping. Just leave it," he said. "It's still raining, so forget it. Go pack a bag, we're outta here!" While I packed, he drove Shari back to her Grandmother's house and dry shelter. It was nine o'clock in the morning. He fed the dogs upon his return. We abandoned ship.

Ever wonder what you would grab during a fast get-a-way? Now, I knew. Whatever you could find quickly. Many things lost importance instantly. Ronnie told me to take a few changes of clothing. I could only guess that we would not be coming back real soon. We packed the car and drove off, slowly. The streets were flooded and cars were stalling out left and right. We had never seen such a water surge on these roads. Tears were now streaming down my husband's face, too. It was all so overwhelming. We fled to Steve's (his boss) house. He had extra bedrooms. It was dry, with running hot and cold water plus a generator. Heaven!

Steve was glad we came. He said he would have been upset if we had not felt comfortable enough to stay there. We were friends also. (Good thing since we ended up staying through mid-December. We didn't get electricity until the end of November.) I had no idea what everyone else did for the remainder of the day. I crashed. I was mentally and physically exhausted.

That evening we watched a video. "Ground Hog Day". I kid you not. How apropos! It was still funny. Sure, I could laugh now. I was dry. That house was dry. There were lights and fans. My own house was a distant memory, surreal.

A couple of Steve's friends stopped by. One asked, "Does anyone want to play Monopoly?" We all exchanged "yeah right" expressions. Ronnie asked her "Can I buy a roof if I play?" I joined in, "How about Water Works? That's what I want." "How about the Electric Company?" someone without a generator chimed in. I think she got the message. No we didn't want to play. Look, after two hurricanes we could be as sarcastic as we dared to be. We were all in an "I don't give a shit" mood.

Saturday September 16th

This day was very important to Ronnie. We hadn't had a vacation in two years and we were supposed to be flying to Margarita Island, off the coast of Venezuela, finally. The room was paid for, it was just waiting for us, with all of the conveniences we were then lacking. The airport was not open yet and we had not booked our tickets, for reasons too numerous to mention. The rainfall, apparently stubborn, would not cease and desist.

Ronnie was sporting a very determined look. Though he didn't want me to go back into our house he took me there to pack for our vacation. I was skeptical, not believing we could carry this off and actually get it all together on time. We had had an overwhelming two weeks, the tension was mounting and we were very close to the breaking point.

The house was worse if that was at all possible. There was more water than from the previous hurricane, everywhere. Things I thought might have been saved had given up the ghost. "Whatever", I thought to myself. I moved with speed and precision. We instructed the housekeeper to feed the dogs while we were gone. We had stocked up on dog food before the hurricanes, but if that ran out they could have as much corned beef hash as they wanted to, as far as I was concerned.

Ronnie dropped me off at Steve's to organize our luggage while he staked out the airport for a flight. Remarkably, he booked us on a flight at five-forty-five that afternoon. I was truly amazed at his tenacity, although we didn't have confirmation for the connecting flight or a room reservation as a back up. Off we went. Our quest for dry weather would not be deterred. The plane took off for Curacao. Either that night or the next day we would fly to

Venezuela, change planes again, then continue on to Margarita Island. We would arrive only one day late for our luxury accommodations.

The plane landed at seven-thirty. I felt better already. Ronnie looked better already. There wasn't a flight available that night so we had to go in search of a hotel room. First we found a taxi. Even now, when I recall how that man drove, I get a nervous tic. Speedy Gonzalez took off like a bat out of hell. My window was down, so my hair was standing straight up above my forehead and my lips were plastered to my teeth. He tailgated each car, leaving maybe six inches leeway. My eyes were glued to Ronnie. He shrugged and shook his head in disbelief. At this point, nothing much phased him. Craziness seemed to be cast as our shadow.

The closest hotel to the airport was booked but the taxi driver recommended another place. I told him to have the front desk verify that the next hotel had a vacancy. They did. Off we went again. The driver said that it was twenty-five minutes away. Yeah, right, not with him driving.

Halfway there, do you know what happens? No, not an accident. Worse. It started raining! I had seen what could be lightening but tried to convince myself it was the tracking lights from the airport. In lieu of crying, I laughed, hysterically. My husband was worried about me. We arrived in fifteen minutes, windblown, yet in one piece. Inside the room we had I.O.L. (instant on lighting), a television, a bed and a bathroom. There was nothing to write home about, only the essentials. Except for one. I'm afraid to tell you. All right, there was no hot water. I really was in the twilight zone. First the rain and now no hot water. We could have stayed home for this. Upon further inspection I realized that there weren't any washcloths either. Well, why the hell would you need washcloths since you didn't have any hot water anyway? "I can't do it tonight. Tomorrow, tomorrow I will take a cold shower, not now," I said resignedly.

I was definitely at my maximum for non-amenities. At home after the hurricane was one thing but now we were paying for room and board with no hot water.

We were starving because we only had a small sandwich on the plane. It was sad, some kind of mystery meat on a dry roll. I checked with the front desk and inquired as to where we might get some "grubbage". "All you have to do" she began to say, "is go half a block to this late night store. They serve hot food." This may not appear so bad, but… I peered out of our one window and I smacked my forehead in desperation. "What is it, the view?" Ronnie asked. "No, not that. Not that the view is good. It's pouring rain and lightening out there. I'll starve. I am not going out in that," I replied adamantly.

I turned the television on. We didn't get any English speaking channels but we watched it anyway. What the hell, let's live on the edge. I must share this one commercial that we saw. It started off with a shot of a woman in a restaurant reading a menu and the waiter pointed to an item, thereby making his suggestion. She shook her head in agreement. The waiter returned with the meal and held it out for the woman to see before he placed it on the table. The camera then cut to goats grazing, looking oh so very cute. The next shot was to the slaughterhouse, the goats had been killed, skinned and cleaned with their heads still on. Then they showed the supermarket where the chef was buying the goat meat, followed by a scene with him in the kitchen cooking this delicacy. They finally cut back to the restaurant and to the woman who was sampling the finished product. She smiles, mmm good. Wow! This was surely truth in advertising. I personally thought it was just a wee bit too much truth for my liking. Now I was scared to watch any more television, so we hit the sack.

We woke up at six-thirty in the morning starving and not for a cold shower either, if you get my drift.

We repacked, got dressed and went in search of something to eat. Nothing was open. There was someone at the front desk so we asked where we could get some coffee, at the very least. She showed us to a windowsill with a towel on it. We were talking serious class here. There were cups, coffee, sugar and Cremora neatly arranged. After five minutes, we still couldn't figure out where the hell the hot water was. "Either I am really stupid or it's too early in the morning and I'm not functioning yet. Would you please go ask her where the hot water is before I kill someone?" She returned with a knife and stuck it into some doohickey on the cold water cooler, and said, "it's broken". "Well, why the hell didn't she tell us that when she first showed us where the damn coffee was? It's me. It's all me. It must be. I must be the one from another planet. There can't be this many spacey people living on earth," I said.

The night before we had arranged for Speedy Gonzalez to pick us up at the hotel that morning and transport us to the airport. You could hear him racing toward us from a couple of blocks away. My stomach was in knots again. "Please God, let us make it to the airport in one piece." Maybe when we got there, we could relax for a few minutes before our flight. We got there quickly, of course, and all in one piece. Thank you God.

Our flight proceeded without any further drama, what a relief. Of course, we knew it couldn't last. Once in Venezuela reality set in. Everyone was speaking Spanish and we didn't speak much. I had my reply down pat "English, please, no hablo español." I did remember that much from high school. We made our way to the terminal,

Hurricanes, Paradise and Fairy Tales

picked up our luggage and headed to customs. Leaving this area, Ronnie was instructed to push a large red button located on a column in front of us. Ronnie pushed it. Nothing happened. We looked up and down, left and right, and all around. Nothing. "Go ahead through" we were directed with a hand gesture. We both looked at each other and Ronnie said, "What the hell does that do?" "I don't know, take your picture? Maybe it's a really, really fast X-ray machine!", I said.

We caught up to a woman sent to the plane to assist people with connecting flights and handed her our tickets. She looked confused. Soon, she had gathered about five other people. They were in a huddle and examining the tickets like they were suffering from a contagious disease. From their facial expressions, I gathered that no one knew where we were to go. Well, thank goodness the person they sent to assist us was so capable and knowledgeable! "I am still an alien." Ten minutes later they all figured out that we had to go one terminal over for our connecting flight. You would have thought that it was across the country, not five minutes away. We confiscated a skycap with his trolley and walked the short distance to the next terminal. At the ticket counter the agent spoke English, thank God. He told us the gate number we were leaving from and we browsed through the airport until our flight was called. While wandering around, I spotted a fight monitor and double-checked our departure gate. It was changed, good thing I had looked. We went to the new gate and waited. Then we heard an announcement that the gate number was changed again, we rushed to that one. Then another announcement stated a different gate. All of the passengers gathered up their belongings and went there. No, we were not through yet, they changed the gate one last time and we all rushed back to one of the gates where we were all previously gathered. I could swear that there was someone looking at us saying "watch this," as they made the change in the departure gate and then watched us scurry back and forth like assholes. Help!

As a matter of course (a very difficult course), we arrived at Margarita Island. I thought the taxi driver in Curacao was bad. Now my heart was in my back pocket. I saw a red light up ahead and he was not slowing down. I looked at Ronnie, my eyes were wide and he could tell the question without my asking it. For those of you who can't imagine my face, the question (of course) was "is he going to stop?" Ronnie shrugged. Sometimes, I just want to smack him. The driver looked quickly from left to right and flew right through the light. I closed my eyes. Here I go again, "Please God, let me get to the hotel in one piece." He has to be sick of hearing from me and I also think I am using up too many of my "Please God, if we could just" allotments for silly stuff. The hotel appeared at last, maybe a mirage? I just wanted to get to my room, turn on the television and relax. The room was not ready yet. Were they not expecting us yesterday? We waited at the bar in the lobby for an hour. "Hello! People, don't you know I'm on the edge?"

The room was finally ready. It was gorgeous. Fantastic view, spacious and most importantly - hot water. I tried that almost immediately. Unbeknownst to me, Ronnie had scouted out a store in the lobby and bought a couple bottles of wine (who knew?) and assorted beverages. There was an ice machine down the hall and he made a few trips. We didn't have a fridge so we improvised and used an empty garbage pail filled with ice as our "wine bucket" and fridge. Ice. Ice. Ice. We had more than we could ever use right at our fingertips. "Heaven. I'm in heaven." Our thoughts went once again to St. Maarten with an ice shortage. We threw out some ice for those who couldn't be there to share it.

(You know how the guys pour out some wine or liquor for their friends that aren't there).

Room service seemed like the way to go tonight, we stayed in and relaxed. We had good food, cable television (in English), air-conditioning and hot water. What more could you ask for?

During the next few days we unwound by one of the many pools and read and swam and tried to put all of our too recent traumatic experiences temporarily behind us. We were even succeeding until one couple, Liz and Claude, overheard us speaking English and were relieved that they had found someone else that spoke English too. As it turned, out they had been originally booked to go to St. Maarten for their honeymoon, but were rerouted to Margarita Island. We shared our escapades with them, at their request. We described the whole island and why they should return in a year or two, depending on when they could get away.

*St. Maarten/Sint Martin is the gourmet capital of the Caribbean

*Best of both: Dutch and French

*Friendly people

*Fabulous beaches

*Relaxed atmosphere

*Great night life and Casinos

*Duty free shopping

*English spoken everywhere

*Overall the greatest island in the Caribbean

I think we sold them. They can't wait to visit and neither should you!

Now I can finally understand people that don't want to relocate but inhabit flood areas, earthquake zones or any other disaster prone territories. It takes a great deal of courage to pick up the pieces and start all over again. Before I couldn't fathom it, now I can relate.

St. Maarten, my home: Fairy tale, I don't think so.

Hurricanes, maybe.

Paradise, definitely.

Wood off right side of roof-replacing it with plywood.

Hurricanes, Paradise and Fairy Tales

My bathroom ceiling

Airport Rd-with boats leaning over it

Cloud Room Restaurant

Hurricanes, Paradise and Fairy Tales

My backyard 2weeks after hurricane

Food Fair Supermarket

Front yard two weeks after hurricane

Front yard-two weeks after hurricane Luis.

L-shaped apartments

Telephone Company-Landsradio

Our house

Cement wall buckling after Air-conditioner blew out of the wall.

Aerial view of hurricane of Luis. St. Maarten is circled

Zinc that was ripped from the roofs.

Kim Norris Samuels

"Zinc tree house"

Hurricanes, Paradise and Fairy Tales

L-R: My brother Keith, Ronnie and Kim
Wedding Day

Kim Norris Samuels

Top L-R- Kim and Ronnie
bottom L-R- Ron Jr., Shari, Jeffrey
Family Portrait summer 1995

About the Author

Kim Norris Samuels is a writer, comedienne and entrepreneur. She grew up in Queens, New York and then lived in St. Maarten, in the Caribbean, for 10 years. She has a 22-year-old son, Jeffrey, living in New York.

Now residing in California, she performs stand-up comedy and has her own business "HaveYouLostYourMind.com". Her specialty gift basket line currently includes PMS, Menopause and Stress Less Gift Baskets!! Her one of a kind silk and dry flower arrangements currently adorn hundreds of homes and some conference centers across California.

Afterword

2003

Ronnie and I are divorced but not because of the hurricane! He currently resides in New York with his daughter, Shari. We remain very close friends. On a sad note: His son Ronnie Jr. was killed in New York in May of 2001, he was 21 years old. This remains unsolved.